Alphabet Year

Alphabet Year

Devon Miller-Duggan

RESOURCE *Publications* · Eugene, Oregon

Resource Publications
An Imprint of Wipf and Stock Publishers
199 W. 8th Ave., Suite 3
Eugene, OR 97401

www.wipfandstock.com

PAPERBACK ISBN: 978-1-5326-0308-2
HARDCOVER ISBN: 978-1-5326-0310-5
EBOOK ISBN: 978-1-5326-0309-9

Manufactured in the U.S.A.   01/03/17

This one's for Miriam.

Contents

Acknowledgements

I am grateful to the following journals and their editors for publishing these poems (sometimes with different numbers):

Apeiron Review, Disorderly Abecedarian 10: Beware
Birds Piled Loosely, Proper Abecedarian 17: Belief
    Disorderly Abecedarian 18: List
    Proper Abecedarian 18: Divorce
    Disorderly Abecedarian 20: Guide
    Proper Abecedarian 20: HaShoah
Cider Press Review, Disorderly Abecedarian 3: Blasphemy
The Cresset, Disorderly Abecedarian 6: Hidden
Gargoyle, Disorderly Abecedarian 5: Calendar
Hollins Critic, Disorderly Abecedarian 12: Cup
Ink & Letters, Disorderly Abecedarian 16: Jive
    Proper Abecedarian 16: Flora
Kestrel, Disorderly Abecedarian 24: Wedded
Rain, Party & Disaster Society, Proper Abecedarian 4: Eleven
Rappahanock Review, Proper Abecedarian 1: Turns
    Proper Abecedarian 6: January
Red Paint Hill, Disorderly Abecedarian 19: Kisses
Rock & Sling, Disorderly Abecedarian 4: Kenosis
    Disorderly Abecedarian 8: Theology
    Proper Abecedarian 8: Introversion
Whale Road Review, Disorderly Abecedarian 2: Return
White Stag, Proper Abecedarian 7: Drowning
    Proper Abecedarian 21: Tempest
    Proper Abecedarian 23: Cloud
The Windhover, Disorderly Abecedarian 1: Beach

ACKNOWLEDGEMENTS

My further thanks go to the bag of sand mold letters that started this all; to my husband, Seamus, my first and best reader, always; the crew of Friday Nite Writes; the good people of the Thomas Parker Society Reading in Santa Fe (especially Jeffrey Overstreet for the best response to a poem I am ever likely to enjoy), and the Glen Workshops for being the ground on which these poems found their feet. Marci Rae Johnson is an acute and fearless editor who found an arc I had only vaguely sensed.

Disorderly Abecedarian 1: Beach

Querulous weather—rain on the ocean flattening sky—
indicators shifting breeze to breeze,
nerving blue beyond the pool—
voluptuary bubbles at one end, stillness at the other.

Menace in a kind of white
obligates nothinging.
Proposition: lines run—shore, dune, storm fence, grass, sidewalk, street, veins.
Zones of keeping or tending—
unfold, unfurl, unwind, unmove, unblur.

Ribboning sound from a child or gull.
Choice-broken hearts everywhere anyone older than a child.
Harvesting rest, breathing in salt.
Xeric heart unfilled, but sufficed.

Yenning dries the ground.
Kilter, off-kilter, on-kilter—presence of absence of welcome.
Fidgeting in the throat instead of speech
anatomizes emotion the way a raccoon washes its hands.

Walk away. Walk toward. Walk over. Walk.
Blithe as dying.
Joss for living.

Syncopy in the sky again—breeze intent, though.

Grind down into sand this heart. Push iron rod in and wait for lightning, for
    storm-made glass.
Love you can dig out with your hands.
Elision of sympathy and lightning—hard as pyrex hearts—
damage that pays the tithe—
torqued branches, wild transparencies.

Proper Abecedarian 1: Turns

And fall & the light tasting of good scotch, like
belief you don't even need to swallow before it lights your tongue.
Catching up. Coming back. Cleaning off. It's okay—you
dove fingers-first into the blue pool summer. Climb out.

Ends. Hinges. Folds (mountain, valley). Turning. Summer's
fainting from her own heat,
grating her bare toes on sidewalks, self-abrading for penance.
Here the light pours like waking, even as it shortens. Dirt
inherits the leaves it fed.
Just as after harvesting, it's good to cut things back to ground.
Kin to air all summer, your skin remembers separateness.
Limber all summer, your skin recalls contraction.
Much presents itself, absents itself—like family or
nerves shifting sequence—firing or frosting
or fluttering your fingers, your skin, leaves. Hinges all manifest in skin,
plain skin against the plain surface of shift—
quieting the way deer quiet before bending to feed. Air
rounds on us, carves us a cave to wear,
so wound about you—
too hungry for love,
unknowing what we knew, yet
voluptuary as eiderdowns,
weathering the bustle and turn,
xerosis of leaf and ground, then frost killing rot.
You can love your skin again because it requires you cover it,
zealous for keeping close.

Disorderly Abecedarian 2: Return

Fainting sky today pulls at
ground, trying to find color.

Why is saw blade made?
Zig-sag of teeth against
my grain, my gain, my rain, my rein.

Nailing words on trees in the forest, leaves
susurrate like pages, but can't read for themselves.

Trembling upward, wing-over-wing, all the birds called home,
Halving the music, having it fly upward with them, they
bother the stratosphere with all warbling and winging—
quilling sky.

Xanthic eyes
pored over every memory of you. Poured myself. Poored my own memory
operating away from itself.
Kindling catches, but there's no more wood for this fire. This fire
exacerbates the cold,
cakes itself all over these hands
until they're not hands.

Re-enter. Something can be worked out.
Justification by feint, by faint, by fifth, by filth.

Love me past
& forward, but not now. Now I'm
demon for saw-teeth & nails
instead of words. When we were
younger we read poets, we were bright
versions of our jaundiced selves.

Xanthic (adj.) acidic yellow

Proper Abecedarian 2: Possibility

. . .& while everything else was rapt watching angels
bother the air with their wings—those
caked-on-lights' glory/fire/stormwind: signifiers of not-
demon, surely-Other, surely-newsbringing, fear-
exacerbating (as if we didn't tremble enough),
faint-faced, trumpet-voiced. While all that's
ground-(maybe even water)-view, what shape messengers
halve the distance between birds (bats? bugs?) and heaven? What blasts
    "ANGEL!"
instead of WINGS? What intermediary
justification of bird's being
kindles the awe of unwinged creatures
loosened from birth from the un-numinous surface?

My havoc, my hectic, my hamshackled harking: I'm
nailing questions on the innocent blue,
operating my own weighted machinery,
poring over the hagiographies, hoping for
quaver up the back of the neck; for
reentry of revelation or reverence to order:
"Susurrate the air, make liver, lungs, gut, heart
tremble recognizably.
Until tremble, until susurration, until quaver—some
version of supplication: think light into someone else's hands."

Why should the beasts of the air have need of angels? Their
xanthic eyes already see everything as they
zig-zag the air like feathers falling, like leaves, like messages falling.

Disorderly Abecedarian 3: Kenosis

Returning from church or the cliff-edge, she spread her arms.
Meanwhile, the others lay themselves down along the shore.
Perhaps selchies. Perhaps for every animal, there is a tribe who can remove
    their skins.
By their skinlessness, by their dreams, by furtiveness—
how they might be known.
Nay bloodworm, nor buzzard can know which of their sisters,
whether any of them chooses, whether each alive thing is
xylem in its soul—tough, fibrous, hard to cut
down, to be nourished by.

Love, some find themselves reaching out of their own skins,
each toward sentience, speech, walking, or longing to
gather themselves only ever with themselves
again, again, against & among
or away into a second nature.

For all flesh shall in their second selves see new gods,
certain of them will walk and walk
to find hiding places for their first skins, a universal
kenosis, all walking away from the divinity of first being,
unraveled until only humans. Leaving, then, only the trees:
justice and judge
zenith and zendo.

Yet the bloodworm, the single unstinging jellyfish, the krill
vent themselves back into their unskins,
quiet again.

I cannot find my own first skin.
Some other godling fills it, fails it.

Kenosis (noun), Christ's relinquishment of divinity in becoming human.

Xylem (noun), water-conducting tissue of woody plants.

Proper Abecedarian 3: Eleven

Again: Poppies & Flags for a war whose soldiers gone
by into the bield of forgetting remembrance forgetting. I am not
certain how spring bulbs' leaves bayonet up through soil without grinding
down their tips, raggeding them like dried blood.

Each eleven seemed sufficient
for peace. Bones and old shells still push through French soil, ragged as dry
    blood.
Gather, Old Soldiers, 100 years & the same war push up bloodied, same
how same millions, row on row. How bulbs lance upward; spring.

I learned to recite "In Flanders' Fields" in 8th grade. Did
justice best I could. It's all armistice,
kenosis, each soldier relinquishing divinity, each
leaf within bulb gives up milky safety of sleep, pushing upward.

Meanwhile: Omaha, Nagasaki, Pusan, My Lai, Rwanda, West Bank, Helmand—
nay bloom in 100 years not red—
or genocide, genocide, genocide, cleansing, genocide—forced kenosis.
Nay bloom in 100 years not red.
Perhaps this time. Perhaps un-red blooms spear through some spring.

Quiet as rows of white stone—
returning bulbs, rows planted wrong season, heads down.
Some numbers: 11/11/11; 21 (years not at war); 86,600,000 (deaths in I&II)—
    always come down
to one & one & one & will

until Ground demands ploughshares, & gods require no bloodcleansing.
Vent-able—everything that lives can be pierced.
Whether anything survives kenosis, beyond keening, breaking apart even
xylem, draining fluids until even wood weeps.

Yet more. Yet poppies & bloodgrounds.
Zenith, n. The peak at which lesson spears ground, unshredded, blooms.

Bield (noun), shelter or home. Archaic.

Disorderly Abecedarian 4: Calendar

November courts martyrs—birds die, women exhaust themselves.
Xylology: The study of wood, not trees. Study of corpses, not being
torn from corpses. Hagiography: Writing the corpse.

March & May—the only month-names meaning something more. Well,
    August.
Grating, grunting, each day does both.
Zephyr my heart, three-weathered day, keep

January—the old year's corpse lingers,
elements disbursing into crystals, into "ask
wooden-heart, the puppeteer, ask what to make."
Can I leave? The house's layers of air
keep thinning. The closer layers
have their own hands.

September resurrects the year, which leaves its tomb, a
bundle of fetid rags and empty pages.

December binds the pages.

October's had breath to write. It will all
revisit the place where the grave re-opened, no
love safe, no longer named.
Yes, someone can leave, something's
unbound, something of
value, like a pebble on a headstone, not exactly gem, not
quite growth, not quite quiet.

August's the witch-furnace—stirring the huge pot
in the fire the air keeps feeding.

February brings nothing to the table.
Put each in its own booth to wait.

Xylology (noun), the study of wood.

Proper Abecedarian 4: Ferguson

August & its burning done. Come snow. Come winter, come
bundling. Yet burning—cities and the shuttered bodies of black humans.
Can black not be the darkness of white hearts? Can
December be instead Waiting-upon-unfearable-births,
elementary un-killing, elementary un-beating, on allchildren children of light?
February & its raised hands. Black lives matter. Raised signs. Black lives
grate against white fear & their own. Black lives
halved, quartered—thrown at, thrown out, thrown against, thrown
in like feed for the caged.
January & its already-failures, its surrendered bodies, its MLK birthday, its
    wounds
kept new-open, uncleansed, unclosed.
La, la, la they had it coming (all of every year). La, li, la. . .
March with its raised fists or switches—any March.
November with its thanks/no-thanks, with Tamir Rice (12-years old) police-
    shot dead.
October with its fallings & departures—any October.
Put the gunsfistsswitches down. Raise the bodies not
quite grown, not quite men, not light enough to save.
Revisit all the violent graves of bodies lightly accounted.
September with its raised belt & *sit down, shut up*—any September.
Torn. This poem between tact & mouths of sharks, this poem
unbound from nothing. This poem white. This poem without body. This poem
    without
value against a raised hand. This poem raises its hand, fisted around nothing
wooden, leather, metal. This poem speaks
xylology—the study of trees, which stand, which rise like black bodies singing:
Yes, we matter. Yes, we voice. Yes, we are trees, tall even when cut down. This
    poem
zephyrs its ungentled breath across the bad years, praying.

Disorderly Abecedarian 5: Blasphemy

Blaspheme: To peel an orange with a hammer—
mantle the ground in blood say the tree is not the mountain.
Polytheist: Dog who loves more than its master, a single child of two parents.
Xenial prohibitions: Do not offer up your children to guests.
Holy: A thing diminished by speech.

Deify = or ≠ defy.
Love = or ≠ deify.

Explain any of this to a broken heart,
god of breaking, god of blood, god of teeth, god of buds.

Omen = or ≠ Oh, men. Amen:
unmanageable—the wings propelling air into lungs,
crux of being = breath.

Negate = or ≠ negotiate, novitiate, neophyte.
Ken this: Ken that I long for bird song, ocean crash, sky-widening
revealing largenesses.

Infidel: To peel an orange with a saw, mantle ground in blood,
flout songs of birds and mammals of the seas & wind in trees.
Sex is the wings of everything that moves the earth—
quill with which maps are drawn,
abundance counted & laid down, laid up into
ziggurats, to hang like gardens upon
twittering of trees, upon
wind's word—
very song from very song—
year spooling into year, green with longing,
just inside the orange's skin.

Xenial (adjective), hospitality to strangers.

Proper Abecedarian 5: Oranges

Abundance: an orange so fragrant it's
blasphemy not to roll it in your hands until they're pregnant with oils; scent
crucial to your belief in senses of Christmas.
Deifying your own hands, everything comes back to Christmas,
explaining the scent of oranges as the origin of your theology, your
First-Cause. It could just as easily have been the taste of butter, or light you
     called
God mazing its way through loblolly needles, rubbing the flaked bark,
holy as pushing needles in-and-out of fabric, the promise you made to read
     Anne Frank.

Infidel: who uses a knife on an orange rather than
just letting its pulp and oils gather beneath your nails before you
ken the burst and acid of its flesh by route & reason of your tongue,
lathe with which you spindle the names of God.

Mantle your hands in any perfume that'll mask the smell of mortality:
Negation = or ≠ negotiation.
Omen = or ≠ open to interpolation, implication.
Polytheist = who cannot conclude whether God is kin, skin, pith, flesh, or seed.
Quill = verb = the winding of threads in order to weave. And to weave is to

reveal: there is a body beneath the cloth, window behind the hanging—
sex embroidering names & perfumes before,
twittering & grinding itself in & out of the fabric like it was god,
unmanaging the Whole once oranges sweetened up,
very skin from very skin, very skin for very skin. Or
wind blowing that labyrinth-drunk light through those pines,
xenial & straining even as it found you,
years too early, well before oranges or angels, when all you wanted to build:
ziggurat after ziggurat of color, trying to reach.

Disorderly Abecedarian 6: Beware

Monsters have been known to take large bites from the moon with their
xyphoid—god-grinding-size—teeth. It's because they're
both everywhere & nowhere that they're so grumpy.
Never underestimate the crankiness of creatures
who never know for what they hunger,
dream of nothing but being full. Even
angels have it easier.

So my grandson tells me stars taste like 16 watermelons, moon like 14 oranges.
    It's no
ruse to finagle more time with the video game, it's that he's for-real
gone wherever innocents go before sleep—those places
could believe
"The star fell in my hands and that was crazy!"

Unto where all the monsters gnash their teeth,
quip away at each other's expense—
zeitgeist of monsterdom wants itself to taste like oranges, wants to
inherit watermelons & stars that can be handheld. They
opine on the subject of crossbreeding dreams & nightmares, on monster
love. They love their drippy bits & razory chunks, would
keep however many eyes they have in interesting places, but, see,
yawn or two, there won't be anywhere in nowhere or everywhere for them
forming & salivating. They'll have been forced to
elevate themselves, fluffed up, into another orangey dimension, somewhere,
verge of the watermelon universe, which will, of course, require papers with
    every
jot and tittle neatly inscribed with stolen crayons pincered awkwardly between
    two claws.

Hear the story: Everything falls into someone's hand; it's always crazy.
Pull up a corner of the universe and bundle in. It's for the best.

Xyphoid (adjective), bony.

Proper Abecedarian 6: Sixtieth

Angels have been known—godsome creatures
both god-breathed & sum of the distance between.
Could we get over wanting and dodging them?
Dream them bursting from the rinds of watermelons?
Elevating cross-dimensional musics into seed and syrup?
Forming barricades like rinds around this fruit on which we live?

Gone, gone—all my ghosts. The grandmother I could always almost
hear, the grandfather I could clearly smell, the father I could never
inherit the way a star might fall into my arms—not one
jot of visitation or vibration that might
keep me apart from my own death or
launch me toward sweetened belief, even complicated inhabitation, shield &
monsters at the same time, those not-entire voices/visibilities keeping me
never earthbound, never—they hinted—maybe mortal until now. I therefore
opine myself the baby in the still seed in the rind in the sweetness no more.

Pull toward the end. Was I then before monster or angel? Keeper of ghosts &
quips—small things I knew I knew. Whose
ruse was it? Sweet fruit, I smelled it everywhere
so long. So long, my ghosts. What is it—to be left without
the wings, or smoke-in-your-eyes eyes, or lips always forming
"Unto" and "Shalt" and "Rise" and "Long," promises prone to blaze up from
verges, but not explain. Now I'm cars sliding on snowy roads—
who shall make song or vision of that? 2 cars, 1 bus, and all alive-o.
Xyphoid days—down to the bones and it turns out they won't make flutes.
Yawn and the whole sky fills your mouth, or the car stops in time or in
zeitgeist, which offers itself as replacement sweetness.

Disorderly Abecedarian 7: Going

Unsaid. So much goes that way. Such
quartet that can't agree on music. Halfway through every piece they
elide the final notes. Like
zipper on a body bag left open over one eye. Like
xaxsis, so that every line pushes into another dimension. Like
ontological profusion. Like four leaves saying "luck" because they're rare,
your unsaid words fill your lungs. You wanted someone to make
beauty out of your life, & I tried. Now we slide
toward your going.

Doves nest in your head; you speak feathers instead of words,
vortices of confusion about what to do.
Love like this scratches away the surface of the heart,
has scratched you away from me, my mother
no longer. Both of us robbed. Both of us never planning to
join this procession. You
raise your hands to me asking me to pull you from quicksand.

Plain kindness is all I have left; plain
cause is no comfort,
ill becomes us both, this laborious, slow
sway toward an end one can't see, the other won't.

Mother, all we go down into sand. See, my
father's already gone.

Weather like this—all ash and frigid rain, nothing
green here except infection.
All we go down, all we go down,
kenning everything that loves us as we go.

Xaxis (noun), an axis in 3-dimensional space.

Proper Abecedarian 7: Sargent

All goes that way—like the lavender on a woman's sash we can never see all at
    once, like
beauty, like
cause, like
dove. Being
elides paint &
father-of-this painting, like
green always speaks flowers, even against blue. Lady Agnew
has wit, beauty, a voluptuous lavender sash, and nothing
ill to say of sitting. Whites
join her eyes and the sash,
kill gravity. She might mistake Sargent's stare for
leer, but it's a joke she needn't share.

Mother of lavender-like-perfumes,
no, like birth-of-seeing—one plane at a time, like
ontological breath—studying being-in-air, being
plain chant and polyphony at once—Archangelic
quartet, songwings, lavender-voiced,
raise and flutter. And you,
swaying into conversation, wonder how she could be *Gertrude,* how
toward that face, that name couldn't be
unsaid. Lavender taffeta, white flurry, French chair—
vortex into her eyes,
xaxis. You are not changed.

Your breath, though, is white ruffles. Her dangling hand—
zipper, opening & closing time, breath, organdy. Ravishing.

Proper Abecedarian 8: Cosmos

Also ekphrasis: yolk-yellow petals cut from light,
berthed above against hardbright blue.
Certain angles offer sure relief or sure danger. Even
dung looks upward, even snow sinks & rises, eventually
evanesces itself springward—froth of white sighing toward filth, breathing into
froth of petals: school-bus-yellow crocuses, yellows of narcissi burst from
    winter
graves glee-drenched, having
had their gravid hibernations. We
infer the lens lay her beneath these cosmos, their
junctures of overlapping petals seeming ready to
knock against the metaled blue, stems
limber & ready to make the stretch, so
much necessity in their insistent arcing, in seen-through petals'
naked layered transparencies, as notes from
oboe, bassoon, & soprano might layer themselves seeking
plenty from the blue, each flower its own
quim of pollen waiting for some bee
rubbing itself against, taking
sugar & multiplication flower to flower. These two
trust each other & the season,
uffish in its colors, dancing every stem's
ventricles around in the light,
which offers up two sulphur cosmos from below flying, almost
x-rayed against the fierce welcoming blue,
yirding blue, consuming them,
zaftig yellow against apostolic blue.

Yird (verb), to bury, (noun), earth. Scottish.

Disorderly Abecedarian 8: Meditation

Plenty humid. Plenty noise. Plenty coolth. Plenty quiet in any
grave. Don't wake the baby or the God. Someone's
had too much worship & not enough attention already. Someone's
certain who's on which list, yet has no idea
which list gets
much attention from the leaves, who
also wonders why some fall, some don't, some fitfully, & some
evanesce, like old gods' tiresome stories, like
zaftig cartoon goddesses we only love for being
froth spilling over the edge of a full glass,
naked as anything being born, as weather, as discarded scripture,
trust, regret, stones, ocean. I'm always
uffish these days, from which you might
infer the barometer's always dropping.
X-rays of my heart would show it cringing, one
ventricle always fist-fighting the other. Everything in the fascia
rubs everything else wrong.
Love tastes like old mulch, dust bunnies—& lives at
juncture of *done* & *left undone.*

Quim: the juncture of *Right Now* and *Leftover.* Someone
knocks you out of step, knocks you over, offers or begs
sugar or babies—*Come on, darlin', play my*
oboe & I'll slide into your
berth & God's in some heaven & all's right, until it's all
dung beetles, no births. The dung beetle's a scarab, too, fit for Pharoah's crown.

Yird or yirdit, it's all ashes & birth, starstuff & breath.

Disorderly Abecedarian 9: Advice

Junk everything.
Frankly, it's the only advice I've got. Even
love. It only gets you
drunk & awkward & stuck, your breath
rank as hairballs & earwax.

Oink. Hungry. Oink. Eat everything. Only advice I've got.
Break it till you make it? Get
Unstuck—even the universe loves the sucking noise it makes.
Gunk lets go. The lovely *SPLOP!* of elephant tootsies pulled free of mud.

Hank of hair in a locket,
wreck of wrack the tide slurps back out.

Struck by light, too dumb with revelation to
xerox anyone else's unmistakes. You're
kink in your own hose,
quick in your own sand.
Yank your own hair into a braid, dunk it in some
ink & write your tragic yarn. Only advice I've got:
Track your own calligraphic road through the scary woods.
Victor writes the history & the vanquished get it in the
neck. Bitch, bitch. Just
muck your own unmythic stables.

Crank less. Crave more. Get
zonked on sky, or the funk of anyway-ness—
elephant in the room gets to sit where she wants, even
on her Pater's antique piano stool.

Pink used to be your favorite color. Long time gone.

Proper Abecedarian 9: Old

Antique wind—none new-made, all circulation, all
breaking out, breaking against, breaking beneath—prepositionally
cranked up air-antics. Have to go somewhere once
drunk on ocean's current & salt-wine. Don't think about the white
elephant in the corner of every room. It won't be there.
Frankly, someone's dear, the elephant doesn't give a damn about your heart's
    corners,
gunk, or gears; there's only so much stuff around & we keep making
hanks-of-hair, bags-of-bones. Something else has to go. It's all
ink on a contract on skin, except for the occasional chunk of space
junk—not enough surely to support constant increase. We're
kink in the system, home-made meteor-crash. We
lie & lie about lying. We
muck it up, cluster-muck, muck-rake then bury, we muckle of malice. Stiff
necked like we're always excited, erecting,
oinking along, thinking we're stars & should be as numerous, turning air
pink with bloodspray—eruption after evisceration after
quick ejaculation of bullets or oil-filth.
Rank-hearted as rotting corpses of rivers or reigns.
Struck by our own hands repeatedly. On
track to leave no tracks. Uninterested in being
unstuck from tar-pits, our hearts. To what
victor could the spoilage go? What
wreck sufficient before we learn:
Xerox benignity, give whatever materializes malignity back to The Supply?
Yank on that thread, can you? No grasp? Just
zonked on want-it-now—like cancer cells, which are also made of star-stuff.

Disorderly Abecedarian 10: Jive

Inside the air outside, humidity
maundering against skin like a tongue in
love with itself. Dear Self, is this an idea of charming
quirk, this endless line of hate-full poems for summer? This
zoo of slime imagery &
urbane whinging. I
defy you: write one encomium where the air's not
bungling its nature with moisty
yellowing droop. You've neither
kith, nor skin who want to listen.

Where's your sense of one-ness with the water molecules all
gossamered into sexy veils,
swansdown and slurp?
As if you had a single
vein that wasn't full of *humid*—you're a sea yourself, sailing your
xebec across the stuff you're made of (moldy sails notwithstanding),
friend (are we?), make peace. Go goopy &
hallow each season with appreciation.

"Putrid" isn't appreciation. It's July, the weather's
reigning; it's supposed to be. You don't see it
crumble beneath your contempt, do you?
Oft, oft you weep, you wimp. The
trouble's not the season. The season's full of locust
jive. & fecundity. Best dance along—beyond fruit yourself.
Endure the spirit of the thing: Lie down, pant, drip.
Noblesse demands: Stop Whining.

Proper Abecedarian 10: Flora

As lurid as the season is, summer doesn't
bungle the senses quite like spring, who tends to
crumble pollen over every surface like streusel on cobbler.
Defy her though you will (and she is surely SHE), you will
endure the yellow drifty air and pollen-sick head for
friendly songs of bird-to-hungering-bird, bee-to-lusting-flower, for
gossamer drifts of breeze across your re-uncovered skin, like sex instructions.

Hallowed be the bulbs thrusting greenswords from
inside their breast-shaped milky bulbs and buds. Hallowed be
jive & jingle of color, the fluff of trees who know no better than to flower pink,
kith jazzed up for kith, lithesome breath
licking at your nostrils. Every thing rises sweetly, or opens like your
maundering heart. You want in spring. In spite of the remarkable
noblesse of borning things doing their duties & pushing out of comfortable
    sleep, you
often understand all this blossoming as burden—like having to say you like
    paperwhites'
putrid winter-forced-false perfume.
Quirk, the ticking off of yet-another-year's
reigning failure—the mother you can neither please, solace, nor let die.

Swansdown air and gibbering flowers
trouble the black heart of your faked
urbane competence. Your mother hates her life. You have no more
veins for her to mine. You don't know
where your limitlessness has gone. You buy her sweets, tulips, dream you're
xebec scudding merchant seas, cargo-rich, heading away from home; dream
    your heart
yellow as mustard, as dandelion, as narcissi, as the piss-smell of a busted
zoo where every animal paces and cries.

Disorderly Abecedarian 11: Watersprites

Under river, near cathedral & gallows, they
mind all coming and going, stray or pound of feet at the edges.
Nor ice, nor summer's anvil sun slows their hunger.
Bindreeds, waterlily stems, water-roots—among,
rhizoming there: See the movement against the current—not quite
haze, not quite solid. They are
about luring. You will believe in their
love's sort, in the silken mobility of their hair & fingers & waists, you will
yarl for kisses & being bound,
tumbled against the rocks with which their river is
gravid with sand & clay.
"Kelpie," your grandmother warned. You only watched light
corruscate the ripples of their hair just beneath surface. Their voices
zel your ears, their hands
flower among the reeds, tending, reaching, promising you will
enter with sudden gills, you will surely breathe
into their water. You
waver like water plants
querling in the currents. You love their
slender faces beckoning, their
open eyes plead. Their smiles
jar—their curved-edge teeth. Your
vanes speak to them
promising them you. Promising you can't
drown, promising. You will know
xerosis, deepest thirst.

Kelpie (noun), Scottish water spirit, beguiles travelers into drowning.

Querl (verb), to twist or curl.

Xerosis (noun), thirst or dryness.

Yarl (verb), to howl.

Zel (noun), an Asian cymbal.

Proper Abecedarian 11: Drowning

About the dream: again
bindreeds tangle your dawn beneath
coruscating light-on-water,
drown you, while you remember water dreams & sex &
enter, finally, your own body; finally
flower. Finally
gravid with petals like a thousand tongues.

Haze comes with waking
into confusing light & warmth, you
jar yourself, bumping against air.

Kelpie, she'll wait. You were dinner. You'll be
lunch. You'll be breakfast. Her dream, her
mind is all for you. Neither your flail,
nor your lungs' air will suffice against her
open eyes & arms, her mouth, her
promise. Your veins
querl with clutched-at-memories; she's planted her
rhizome in your lung's memory—one strand of green hair,
slender as recollection, as choking.

Tumbling from the pool of sleep, still
under the dream's hands, day's
vanes twist in the light, point everywhere,
wavering while you find a direction.
Xerosis after drowning fuddles. Finally skin
yarls awake. The day, your lover, alarms itself—
zel of alarm shocks you back into breath.

Disorderly Abecedarian 12: Theology

Happily, the God settled, letting
unequal creatures uprise side by throat by wing by bloom by
kite. One thing near perfection, another near failure, all
Zion of feeding, being fed, breathing, breaking, breaking as
before the Hand That Made demanded its own perfection, left Itself
mute before Itself. Probably
a rending. Then, an end. Possibly
gift, graft, or gaff—sameness & sameness.
Take water. Salt, sweet, brackish, clean—which closest to ItSelf?

Wall between Creation and Perfection.
Rail between location & translation.
Next, stop. Next, start. Let the made things make themselves. Behold

xenia—one fertility breeding upon a foreign surface,
cutting through one completion toward revision.
Qua evolution: The whole thing's round-heeled, floozy, prone to
sunder one connection, seek another
onto which to splay itself & burrow.

Love's profligate by nature, un-
jailable from field to field to flower to poison.
Is this the intention? Ontology? Promiscuity?
End? Where one bloom begins, another bursts.
You see?
            You question. You watch. You breathe. You breed.

Venture out along the edge. Take in air pushed upward.
Don't breathe it out over the same edge. Turn
purely away, exhale, step toward, toward certain ground. You won't be
forced to stay. You won't be forced to breathe again.

Xenia (noun), the effect on a hybrid plant of pollen from a different strain. Also, a variety of hand-shaped coral.

Proper Abecedarian 12: Introversion

A god settling like radiation from burnt clouds, crookeding everything
before there was anything to become, anything to
cut a mouth-slit into, anything questioning, anything hungering.

Don't pray to settling, for settling. Nor for
end. Nor for voices from above-around. Don't
force company. Who said She wanted a First-Made
gift to do her, asking for her parts, her voice, her
happily busy-touching hands? She
is full of garden & looking, tasting flowers. Why should her listening turn
jail? Why should prison be Casting Out like let-go
kites, nothing but air to live in, nothing but ground to fall toward. He,
lazing, waiting, following, whining about too much to learn, should have stayed
mute, or been thrown—flawed potter's jar—out first.

Next, God of Deserts—so like the Man—always wanting, dropping
onto sand next to Her, like surprises or ladders,
purely noise & discontent. She wanting only to watch sand flow through her
    hands.

Qua multiplication: the First Boys spilled their seed into sand & sand bore
    fruit. She
railed against the thousand thus-begotten daughters' heart-
sundering clamor and birth-cries. She

takes herself off toward water,
unequal to mothering so much,
venturing toward Knowing, toward What Was Beyond, away from the
wall of angels around the womb-garden of Every Thing, away from the sons'
xenia, walking. Walking pattern after pattern into the sand.

You get it? Her walking, her sand-mazes beside the waters, her Zion.
Zion: Stay alone with making.

Disorderly Abecedarian 13: Cup

Kind of wound unhealing. Body not willing. Water not for thirst.
None growing with fruit, what plants live.
Quarellous those who stayed; hungry who left
unknowing how far in all directions the blight. Many died. The King in his
yawl, pulling the lines, deft & unthirsting. For the esoteric procession only, he'd
jumble those left, all living for one meal each day borne in by servants not his,
    while
brute unhunger left him
fisher who ate no fish, like
xerophyte plants—leaves only for grasping water from air, roots for only
hewing to ground. Nothing beyond can
mend. Nothing but wind alive. No spirit
squandered on healing. No thing
love but the rocking of boat on water. Nothing a country. Only
zealots coming with their lusts & queries, leaving
granted nothing, neither wisdom, nor forgiveness, but feasted, never knowing
Cup from which the humming servant gave wine, always wanting to touch
Wound, always afraid of the bloodsalt. No
oath sufficient to their horror. Each another
iteration of ambition, concupiscence, longing, or arrogance, each
vexing the King with keeping him on land. Each more
awkward than the last. Each
ever leaving like husks, like chaff on wind. None to
purify the wound or discern the Cup, all
damned as the land, until the stupid one ignored
tragedy and offered hospitality to his host,
reveling against the dust.

Proper Abecedarian 13: Demesne

Awkward, the unhealing. Suggestion of
brute greeds, a burdensome soul, fouled blood—
cup full-forced against the lips of a messenger.

Damned land. Rock and branch draw
ever in on themselves, cells fighting to consume each other.
Fisher of what? Pardon? Excuse? The one fish who'd drown him?

Grant this: everyday, somewhere, some who
hew to belief in their own deserving, own armor, cut themselves—
iteration of the King—fail to die, but kill their demesnes.

Jumbling the deaths—Rowan Tree, Year-King, Shepherd—all their
kind to blame for the darkness that covers the land &
lays itself down to sleep, Kings' beaten hearts for its pillow.

Mending nothing, lying each in his own waste,
none but castle rock, field rock, tree-split rock to offer
oath, & that oath another emptiness.

Purificators for bandages.
Quarrellous half-beings for servitors,
reveling nightly: bright feast of un-nourishment, procession, recession—

squandered like the Hanged Man—for always ungraved.
Tragedy: the always fathers wounding themselves & laying always waste,
unknowable recoveries—everything choked before still rebirth,

vexed, ignored like fish left live on the bank, like bodies
wound alive in barbed wire left to its bloodwork, like
xerophyte plants encased in vacuum.

Yawl leaves shore, shoves the land away.
Zealot for solace only & not for strength.

Disorderly Abecedarian 14: Allhallows

Trolling the blue-greying sky between black branches,
loving the other-side-wind and yellow-spark street-lamp next road over—
sword unsheathed against the coming dark, visceral against the antlered night.

Yon darkling thrust—thirsting branches, departing sky, starved-yellow light
vie with the wasted day—not-making, neither praying, nor eucharist, nor even
ire against making, prayer, or feast. Nor
zest. Nor tears. Nor sufficiency. Nor hunt. Nor
armor. Nor amor. There must be
moon other side of the house. Any light's still possible.

Castle day: switch pieces on the board—one behind the veil,
dragon-guarded until the graves settle & the Hunt passes,
going forfeit to forfeit, collecting souls & playthings.
X-through-X may multiply to Time, to Sacrifice, to Bulwarks, to Doors,
King banishing kings—Arawn and Arthur both.

Every story unbuckles its greaves, breastplate, helmet. Each list
howls when morning starts, then quiets—
not checked, not winded, not wounded, not choked. Not
blood-bound, relinquished, even by chalice. Not
plunged among the fray, the ancient hunt, the faithful. Not promised.
Untried, unhunted, unsolaced.
Queen of nothing—ungorged—beyond this winded, now-dark sky, though
winged or wingful—jessed, hooded, cage-quiet,
oaf-silent, naught-voiced, confession-swallowing. Safe from
faery's angerish royalty. It's autumn turned; the Wild Hunt's passing, antlers
jutting like whole-tree branches ancient. Stars fade. Allhallow's over; the Hunt
ranges even into Sunday, hungering. I keep close.

Proper Abecedarian 14: From

Armor a form of succorance.
Blood a form of supplication.
Castle a form of brutality.
Dragon a form of angel.
Every form from longing.
Fairy a form of lacemaking.
Going a form of acceptance.
Howl a form of lucidity.
Ire a form of raveling.
Jut a form of credence.
King a form of fertility.
Legitimate a form of deviation.
Moon a form of abnegation.
Not a form of confession.
Oaf a form of solution.
Plunge a form of acceptance.
Queen a form of succorance.
Range a form of enclosure.
Sword a form of unfolding.
Troll a form of interrogation.
Untried a form of seduction.
Vex a form of encroachment.
Wing a form of dragon.
X a form of permanence.
Yon a form of narration.
Zest a form of armor.

Disorderly Abecedarians 15: Guide

Neither rein, nor reign, nor rain, nor dark of history: Those haggy
three were just frowsy birds falling from somewhere; Mackers should have
    hustled them off to
Inquisition. The Dominicans would have known how to
love those crones to death—
barbed kisses, thorned seats, razored sleep.
Except, Macbeth preceded St. Dom by centuries—
ugly ones, dark as cauldrons full of newts, were dust. Mackers: Alpha dog with
zeta heart, & a Wife who even used the word "Screw" to urge regicide.

Part of it had to be the sex. A woman with ambition
Ferments more than dark-age homemade beer. She wants to be
xenogogue, the one clapping her unclean hands: "We're walking, we're walking,
    we're killing."
Gender had something to do with it; it always
winds its way like cauldron steam or spit—laundress & brewer desperate to be
vital, even when infertile.
Red is the color of my true love's hands, corpse the color of my true love's jaw,
yoke the color of my true love's tongue.

Debunk this history: Trees walked. I
mounted my horse, my wife, the throne. I
slighted my knowing, the realm—used my sword as needle, stitched our
quilt of blood & bafflement & battlements. All
along the spiral hill-fort road, butchery as meet for power.
Jangle, jungle, sword, and bungle, sire burn & marriage wrangle.

Catch at least the children as they fell.
Knit them back together—swords as needles. Swords for digging. Swords for
    carving.
Held by their edges, by their butchers.
Occasion: a failure about which poets write. And rite.

Xenogogue (noun), a guide for foreigners.

Proper Abecedarian 15: HaShoah

Along the tracks of trains, along tracks made by hayricks outside Dachau,
barbed symphonies wiring the special air.
Catch what falls from sky on your tongue—black flakes.

Debunk=dragged from sleeping racks to stand in freezing mud to be counted.
Except where camps had no bunks.
Ferment=history=Armenia=Rwanda=denial=remembrance stops nothing.

Gender determining nothing beyond names: one shall be Sarah, one Isaac.
Hold their hands even now, Dr. Korczak. Even now they should be held.
Inquisition=Nuremberg. Evolution=Nuremberg. Promulgation=Nuremberg.

Jangled voices—Beethoven, Goebbels, Brahms, Höss, all the soft vowels of
    Berlin.
Knit bones, rebroken, knit, rebroken. House knit of bones in forest of bones.
Lower: Bunker, grave, bootsole, emptied pot of water soup. Lower.

Mountain of shoes, of gold teeth, of hair (felted for submariner boots), of eyes.
Neither rain—even forty days', nor oceans can wash.
Occasion=27th day of Nisan=Witness. Witness=

part Romani, part POWs, part homosexuals, part farmers, part children, part
    cantors: 11,000,000.
Quilt of memory—a thousand, thousand patches sewn by bleeding fingers.
Red threads: pogroms, Georgia, Decossackization, Anatolia.

Slight of history conceals Ustasha, Sudan, Maya, Indonesia, or doesn't.
Three sentences: Never Forget. Never Again. Never Ceasing. One wish, one
    truth, one lie.
Ugly=the bodies of Nanking, Burundi, Bangaladesh, yet
vital. We must breathe. Are pslams not filled with slaughter after slaughter?
Winding-cloth strips: Belzec, Chelmno, Majdanek, Sobibor, Treblinka.

Xenogogues=Synagogue=guide reminding you *hold your hands up to your face,*
see their work written there.

Yoke the twin oxen History and Confession to pull you over the stinking graves.

Zeta=perhaps there is always a Korczak to hold the childrens' hands.

Disorderly Abecedarian 16: Green

Nothing arrives, scans the crowd for
Anything. But she's not there. She's gone
somnambulant, like balconies and oranges &
entire nights filled with someone's cries:
Zymosis of the night air & the ache &
blear of green, drunken,
curling upward—vines from open mouths screaming. Nothing wants to
mitigate the night, but even stars
quail where orange bursts even beneath
kinder balconies, the railing's
writhen by such twisted light. Nothing leaves. Nothing
harvests Anything, carries her in his arms.

They wanted each other's arms, wanted to
polish rings with long wearing. Air that smelled of oranges turns
vile when the sky's gutted.

Xerxes' spear couldn't reach that skin. Blood
oranges' flesh on Anything's tongue. Her
great love burns the night. Words fall out of the rent sky,
imply there's someplace safe, somewhere she can
love & scrape the pith from the skins of oranges. Missiles
ululate with the air's tongues,
reprise of sand. Filling open mouths. Is this the civilized
yawp? I am as dead as the grass growing from my harrowed mouth?

Due to each of these fallen as due to me, as due to
jury of balconies. Even the iron railing that can't be breached should
fluster with flame, open its mouths and speak vines.

Zymosis (noun), fermentation.

Proper Abecedarian 16: Faithing

"Anything can turn into a metaphor for faith—or nearly," I caught myself saying,
bleary with Lent and making promises I'm not sure I want to keep: *A wave's*
curl can shelter or destroy, shelter & destroy anyone who ventures in.
Due diligence asks what this might mean about the reliable truth of faith.
Entire rivers—banks, rapids, falls, fords, pools, run-off poisons.
Flustery abstractions interpolate themselves: *Time. Hesitation. Absence.*
  Presence. War.
Great trees—their systems of roots, fauna, branches, thirst, seeming death,
  rebirth, death.
Harvest—plowing, sowing, watching, weeding, watching, tending, reaping,
  un-hunger.
(implication there that all things contain the seeds of themselves. . .)
Jury—12 unkindred minds, distracted hearts, flawed apprehensions—12
  witnesses.

Kinder to see it everywhere, this evidence via abundance?
Loathsome to feel it everywhere lighting the world to blandness.
Mitigating the slapped child, the burned air, the shattered soldier? Mitigating
nothing more often than not. Nor void, nor noise, nor lash, nor fasting.
Orange as oranges. Faith-full as faith. Fishy as full nets.
Polishing its own mirror. Sorting its own coin. Shall I
quail before, stand before, splay myself open before it?

Reprise: Credo, in all things done and left undone. Credo like a
somnambulant, steady on stairs she doesn't know she climbs. As
they sew, so shall they wrap a child in shroud, shroud a seed in soil. They shall
ululate, as the air burning the light wavers and seems Other.
Vile, evil, live—conditions leading to metonymy: I am not shit. I am dust. I am
writhen; branch and root, sap & leaf all Faith, all fault.

Xerxes, about whom no sources agree—builder, ravager, fortunate, betrayed—
  is faith, is

yawp, is plainchant, poly-history, his story. Mine: drystone wall, rough square
    of ground where
zymosis leads to fragrance, leads to vinegar or wine, & I drink what's offered.

Disorderly Abecedarian 17: Ploughshares

"Judgement by declaration," she said, the discussion
ruminating from St. Paul to sandwiches. She
oblivious to other versions so long as she remembered:
suss out more than one version of grey (cool, warm, French), & not
cuss too much at her opponents'
gussied up statements of fear & loathing over our/their
quagmire du jour. Thinking of vampires & the applications of
xylotherapy, saddened recalling her opponents were human—no more
venal, mostly, than she—possibly no more
narrow-opined. Still,
hard stakes stuffed up under a left rib might silence a noise or
two: the tubas of opinion, the oboes of grief. The
welt is always with us, late & soon.
Indeed. In deed. In dead.

Finch at my feeder, do you make war?
Pinch the world in your beak, squeeze until it shatters—
extravagant waste? Page after page from this my
atlas tears itself free & wings into the air, burning. Even-
keel becomes ever-keelhauling, turning the best ideas into raw
meat she never would swallow. Even she couldn't
beat her own heart into ploughshares. Her own
dumb, heat-seeking missle.
                    We could make a new
zodiac in which each house was a war. & define
love as what happens in between, on cusps.
                    We could, she offered,
undo the first fist clenched in the
young world, coax each finger free of its intentions.

Xylotherapy (noun), the use of woods to treat disease.

Proper Abecedarian 17: Belief

Alternatively, we might call it malarkey,
beat at it with our eyes or reeds,
cuss at it like we're prissy (Dag-nabbit! Jeezle-beezle! Peachpit!), say it's just
dumb and tell it if Belief were a dog we'd been lavishing with
extravagant treats & pastel-gemmed collars, we'd turn on it, kick it. If it were
finch-that-broke-its-neck-against-window, we'd bury it. If it were
gussied-up-hat-we-pinned-on-twice-a-year, we'd feed it to goats. If
hardwood, we'd swear at it & keep on banging the nail into the knot.

Indeed, were we comfy in it, even then we'd pick fights with St. Paul, pass
judgement on St. Jesus-loved-me-best-John who goes after Jews. No even
keel worth trying for, just apocalypse & whatever happens if you sit on the
     same rock for years, no
luxuriating in padded pews, just benches made for no-one's back, no
meat, or too much, too much gristle for human teeth to sort.

Narrow or broad, all roads paved with glass & salt, & all feet bare.

Oblivious to all this blare and roil, Belief
pinches itself awake from your dreams. You'll never track via
quagmire, nor by
rumination: chew, chew, chew, hoping to
suss out Belief's smell (vanilla? cumin? frog-liver?), Belief's fingerprint (every
     breather's face?),
too empty to find anything by looking inward, iconward.

Undo your own braids. The *malarkey* might be The Matter—
venal, mortal—all paperwafers stuck to the roof of the world's mouth,
welts on a tree's bark—nail marks and someone else's nails-gouging—all of it
xylotherapy = doors for the whole of us to break down or walk through,
young lamb's blood swabbing every creature's lintel. Belief = new
zodiac: we are all of one house, one rising.

Disorderly Abecedarian 18: Above

Astonished, the sky by its ability to spread, like a bishop's billowy
sleep. The Bishop of Blue thumps earth on its head—Confirmation of the
moreness of its whereness & its so-proper
coop in the Great Chicken House, the Universe. Through which it does not so
    much
fly as stay with wings useful only for creating a flap. This will not
elevate sky into Host—another roundness which both flies & does not.

Brew prayers—it's what fermentation does, does it not—release bubbles &
    abundance like
Zucchini gone feral. It's been good summer—bright enough you might have
    found
key of some sort to unlock the chest you folded yourself into, a key
radiating like Grail in the Fisher Queen's hands. But, back in wild blue
ylem: you'd like to think it'd have coughed itself black by now, with all that
jargon we toss up like chaff or confetti; you'd expect
xenoliths springing up everywhere. But still sky lets us through, makes colors.
    Sky's a
witch, bless her round heart, making newts & bug tongues we scratch from
ditches & there she is, not
oblivion at all, but sparks & colored swaths & breastmilk. She's
vestment & geography, raiment & direction for our
pestilential selves. Sometimes we manage the odd
glissando of gratitude, that always ends when we run out of
love, or when our hands get tired. Our hands get tired of knitting
holey sweaters for a planet, holding them up to check the fit. We live in
quandary: do we deserve the sky or does the sky need to be deserved? Clouds
undulate & splatter & swashbuckle themselves for our attention. We
trek along like everything's a mountain, wear our worst burnings like
necklaces bought to speak our names for us.
Indefatigable sky stays where we need & lets things through.

Xenolith (noun), foreign fragment in a rock formation.

Ylem (noun), the stuff that existed before the Big Bang.

Proper Abecedarian 18: Tempest

Astonishing herself by coughing both storm & wine,
brewing a black froth of cloud & wind,
cooping the whole unwieldy fluster in her demesne, she, Island,
ditched the delicate ship, witched weather, pitched forth humans—either
    fallen, or
elevated for being strewn across her skins & fruits. They
flew off waves as seabirds break necks against sudden rocks in fog, choked
glissando of flight. She was There—fabric of the island's
holey flesh—bogs and burrows—
indefatigable as far as the warlock knew. As far as the warlock's
jargon & blather—she didn't mind. He thought himself
key, thought she couldn't read his books made of wood & skin, didn't quite
live except he called her, taught her. He forgot her
mane of weed unspooled to hold his boat together & draw it in, her
necklace of shoals spat to make the storms shy off. He thinks
oblivion—before he made shore she lay nameless,
pestilential—all quagmire, knife-ish rock, parasitic vines, a
quandary of low creatures whimpering in trees, brackish springs. Yet, a thing
radiating *survival*. He failed to see her
sleeve of inlet open itself, never saw her flatten rocks to ease their
trek across the swamps, stayed blind as she pushed berries forth,
unpoisoned springs. Her
vestment he believed he changed with conjuring.

Witch she made of clay and thorns—herself in his image—to get with him a
    wordy
xenolith to bosom when he returned to rule. He called her Island, she called
    herself
Ylem, fashioned fruits & lessons—artichokes, tomatoes, melons
zucchini. He thought he gave up nothing when he left.

Disorderly Abecedarians 19: List

Profess to the bones of your hatred, the sinews of your loves, your
insight where your profession's surely
helps others summit mountains, circumnavigate cobbler's benches, where ere
    they've
felt called. Gather wherever:
tipple dew, salt water, mead, rain, wine. Tip
up your chalices of choice, however
many might slake your green thirst.
Cumber yourself not much with thinking. The world's
glazed with rainwater or grace. The world's
velvet for to clothe yourself. The world's
nature is pushing against, around, through—
defense against lying down unless for sleep or desire.

Jettison the rock in your shoe, burr beneath your shirt, bee in your beret.

Zoom goes the heart—it's after
alteration. It wants more than leaves, bread, velvet, more than
love. Love's a glutton, master,
slaver. Love's fond of cliffs, bridges, cathedral spires. Love's
onset breaches the heart's thickest bark.
Yonder, love's become woodpecker. No matter how you
wander, it's waiting between grains of sand, cobblestones, threads.

Quibble, carp, cavil, nit-pick, pettifog—you're on
road perpetually, & beside the road always
xenogamy going on everywhere there are bees: Love's
bigamy, polygamy, herd. Every path crosses another somewhere. Love's a
kennel, a waiting room, a too-often plowed field. Love's
elders laugh themselves silly, or puke every ten minutes, or take up knife-fights.

Xenogamy (noun), cross-fertilization.

Proper Abecedarian 19: Divorce

Atlas = Book of the World = approximate pictures of What Is. What is
bigamy if not marrying ourselves/oursouls & the world. We
cumber ourselves with both & trying to keep both fed. There is no
defense for 148 dead 12/16/2014, or 148 dead 4/2/2015, no
elders between the young & gunmen divorcing by way of bullets. None holding
    guns
felt their own souls divorce the world, fissured
glaze of the vessels that held their own marriages of soul & World, no
help for the students, no help. No
in-sight, just bullets to feed some godlet,
jettisoning, severing, breaking open, breaking down. Turning schools into
    killing
kennels, charnel houses which feed nothing but graves,
levering souls from young vessels, so
many, & the same number (Kenya, Pakistan) as jet passengers over France.
    What
nature evolved this? Some were promised escape for calling parents at the
onset & explaining why others must die. Then killed. I
profess Kenya. Pakistan. France. I looked as long as I could for any
quibble, for God's sake, any worthwhile argument about how to walk the same
roads as before one hundred forty eight were killed—
slaver, slave, believer, denier, murderer, murdered, thief, stolen,
tipplers of Godsblood, tipplers of acid, tipplers of milk.

Up in the Kenyan school balcony, a photographer took photo after photo.
Velvety, the lake of blood in which they lay, face-down, camera
wandering over their bodies like a satellite over a continent:
xenogamy by bullet—all their blood, one fruit.
Yonder, where those who fear always love. Yonder, where they cannot touch us.
Zoom in. See how close they lie. Their bodies married to the world.

Disorderly Abecedarians 20: Kisses

Kissing the world again. Again, it's a lousy kisser.
Surely, after 4.54 billion years, this only-planet-with-mouths would quit
yammering long enough to learn how to use its lips; kisses-on-foreheads
    should be
xenium. We're guests, right? We
obey guest rules & you not-quite-sphere-not-quite-pear, our host
beneath our feet/tires/cleats/hands-and-knees obey host rules, yes? But you're
quiescent beneath us, like an unenthusiastic lover,
worth the effort only if you're desperate. Well, there's the food-and-water
    thing. . .

Riches ungold are kisses. World's
venous system pumps nothing about
love, no matter how hard we pucker.
Amber keeps each & every pucker, enclosed &
nude for as long as World is around,
tree rings stop forming, winds'
humble, tectonic plates quiet, & sediments
curdle like cottage cheese instead of housing history. So long will kisses
puddle in the air like humidity, gather & splat, making
muddling of the ground.

Dang, it gets hard to keep walking through pooled kisses, &
Zeppelin of Rescue has caught fire again. The planet's skin's gone
frangible, crumb-able, ground up by our every heel-toe. Kisses coagulate,
garble themselves into a new atmosphere—
infinite sloughing toward cleanliness. Oceans re-become primeval
jelly, fecund with eventual affectionate life. The sky
untells the whole story, while the stars still,
enthralled by the comedy.

Xenium (noun), in classical antiquity, a gift offered to a stranger or an ambassador.

Proper Abecedarian 20: Resin

Amber keeping every & each smooch in honey if
beneath fossil-resin you believe what's caught is sweet, not
curdled life. God's resin; we're flies.
Dang, it looks like whiskey, doesn't it? And dang if we're not easily
enthralled by what seems slow & sweet, promising just a little burn. We're not
frangible by faith, not these our battered hearts—beating, beaten, rhythm
garbling prayer to where you'd think Creation might be
humbled by how much we cry, beg, labor toward that
infinite, or drip nano-breaths thereof. No shocker then, this
jelly the pine trees weep seduces captives made from kisses of belief,
kissing airy cheeks of peace, whatever
levels moments might contain of reason. No wonder we
muddle it: Batter my heart, three-personed God & deep-fry me, Jesus.

Nude we fall into the arms Beelzebub holds out like boiling grease. Nude we
obey the governors, our flesh & ravishers, our selves. Hell might as well be
puddled, smoking oil. We sin; we fry. At least the fly in amber's all
quiescent, all unbothered, all unknotted, as left
riches waiting to be smoothed & worn for pretty or pain relief.

Surely we have loved, would be loved fain, if faintly in spit of
trees—at least they're evergreen, ever awake. We can't
untell the blame & lapse we've witnessed to, the
venous burn of watching blood let in the name of God/not-god/My God, of
worth defined by washed-off hands. Amber, then,
xenium to angels, those ambassadors of cataclysmic change, who leave us
yammering into dirt, drool making cure-no-blindness mud. Not amber, instead
zeppelin we travel in, on which an un-gifted angel lights a match.

Disorderly Abecedarian 21: Blame

Possibly my heart needs to be carved into a grotto, perhaps hammered in place like
roof, perhaps it's meant to be made of heartwood, or
jade. Perhaps it's meant for different dances—neither war dance, nor gavotte, no
tango with its angles & threats. Perhaps it'll eventually
untangle itself from itself. Perhaps learn to be both quiet &
quick (as in, Not Dead). Perhaps it can become, in what time it's left,
homologous to a road, a medium-sized waterfall, an octopus (adaptable),
nematode (tough, simple, easily fed), camel (spits at what irritates). Still,

snickering at the odd good pun helps, though proper
observances do not beckon. A decent
kip now & then will do, the odd good snooze-in-a-box. No riches to
embarrass me once the whole voluptuous business stops. I'm
zombie-heart—all thunk & stagger.

Death's inarticulate or over-explains itself,
girth girdled by a monk's cincture/hangman's rope.
Filth, either way—animate or real corpse, undesirable.
Curve of the scythe, that's a thing of beauty—a waning moon
with a purpose, a tool efficient & splatter-making as
love; as heart-felt. Perhaps I remain
indecisive about whether it's my own heart, ass-deep in
alligators, or awake & see-breathing
vasts of mountain vistas, or still
maidenly & somehow sweet,
boyish in its need to scratch & jump off furniture. I blame the indecision on
xenogenous influences—movies, recurring weeds, tornado warnings.
Yeah, xenogenous voices: God waving while drowning in blood.

Kip (verb), to nap; (noun) a place to sleep; (noun) a bundle of untanned hides from young animals.

Xenogenous (adjective) acquired from a different species.

Proper Abecedarian 21: Ouroboros

Alligator, after all, is just a left-here dinosaur. Or dragon.
Boy, does that bounce around a girl's sense of linear time. Turns out time's a
    nest?
Curved? All the way around. Always, we knew the world would eventually
    consume itself,
death would get itself devoured along with all that in its circle dwelt,
embarrassed in front of itself—expel, expectorate itself back out—
filth & foam swirled on the floor of expectation.

Girth matters—throat's interior girth. And appetite. And growth.
Homologous—dragon, serpent, alligator—all horror-mouthed. Turns out
    creation's
indecisive about survival,
jaded by variety, inclined to grab a
kip while mosquitos & viruses weasel to the front of the line. Turns out
lumbering along like mastiffs & stegosauri can get you wiped out, &
maidenly dithering about procreation (see *Pandas*) gets you ungot, but
nematode squirms along through 25,000 species, all with assholes at both ends.

Observance of ouroboros inclinations (see *Human Brains*) proves they
    meander:
possibly benzene, possibly kundalini, possibly platonic immortality, possibly
    halo. Yet they
quicken nothing, but repeat themselves via their own digestion. And there's no
roof on their eternal returns,
snicker though some might (ever see an alligator eat its own tail?) at
    regurgitation-as-procreation.

Tango, quadrille, do-si-do, waltz—it all goes round & round
untangling the knot by digesting it. There is, I swear,
vastness in such constancy, always eating only yourself, always coming out one
    end or the other
with new skin every time,

xenogenous skin as far as the reptile's concerned—exotic, luscious-smelling—
yeah, just a little lick. It's not like
zombies. Nothing like.

Disorderly Abecedarian 22: Glory

Xenophon, Virgil, Homer, Caesar, Whoever-Wrote-Beowulf: I remand you to
    historical
quarantine. Permanently. For a generation or two. However long it takes for
ring-rattle of swords to stop sounding the doxologies of Warrior Gods. Fort
    wall
bricks dismantle to usefulness, or dissolve into
mud. Beowulf's enemy-arm-bedecked halls feed termites, even after such
effort expended on home décor. Let's find the literary equivalent of a boys'
zenana for all the with-your-shield-or-on-it crap. Only after the gold, Caesar
    was
velociraptor, anyway—just one who could (&, by Jupiter, did) count his
    slaughtered. I
guarantee—wish I could—that a good rest and a nice
klatch—maybe with tea—or even a noisy kibbitz, might overhaul the sword-
    strutters and blood-
fops into organic farmers and tailors.

Pesteration upon them for making the bodies of offspring look noble. Pens
    down; be
nesters, builders, gardeners, painters, healers
jesters (you know—the ones who always tell the truth, but stay sloshed). Let
    their
woes no longer require slaughter, their walking no more cadenced
twos toward blooding, their
undue glories dead or paralytically frenzied as a berserker's eyes. Let there be
    neither
dalliance with body-breaking, nor
slatternly approach to splatter; neither enemy heads in niches by the front
    stoop, nor
ovens. Neither nature split and blinding everything's right order, nor
love of death's harvest.

Cloves & rosemary lay down between buried spearheads, shafts become

arts, or fences for animals, each weapon
its own destruction—
hissy burn of iron gone in the crucible for cooking knives and needles. Let spin
yarns of wool, not Xenophons.

Proper Abecedarian 22: Cloud

Art never helps. Nor prayer. Nor company of women. Nor
bricking shut the door to the grey room. Nor
cloves held against the sore tooth. Nor
dalliance with joys small (sugar) or large (salt waters). Nor
effort. Nor shoving the muscles of the mouth upward. Black Dog's a
fop-bitch of shiny coat, ruffled fur, grinning—fed on fat meats
guaranteeing its healthy teeth & well-being. Or not the Dog & teeth, but
hiss of the Snake in the Tree of Loathing,
its forked tongue drowning your ears surely as Dog chews your heels. Where's
    the
jester when you need barbed truth useful as string-in-the-labyrinth? The
    Bitches, your neurons,
klatch over cups of bile like women whose husbands never listen enough. The
liquefaction of intention sounds nothing like silk. The air, your heart, light,
    sound—all
mud, muck, muzzed like the heat of the Bitch's breath before she clamps down.
    It's a
nester—Dog/Snake/Bog—3-in-1 and 1-in-3—likes it airless & overwoven.

Ovens cannot fire the mud into vessels.
Pestering cannot call the Snake out of your gut.
Quarantine cannot fence the Black Dog.

*Ring the bells that still can ring** only pulls you back when you're halfway down.

Slattern. Slug. Sloth. Slacker. Slow-wit. Slumber-heart. Sloven—you get noth-
    ing done.

Twos: functional/sad, awake/unwilling, sewn/cut, quiet/jangled, earned/
undue. That last: this Bog is undue punishment for drawing breath. This
velociraptor—your heart eating its own young—undue punishment. For
woes written by someone else's hand on your skin, your lineage, leaving you a
    female regiment of

Xenophons—historian-warriors. Watch them stretch the linen out nose-to-
fingertips, measuring
yards for bandages or scrolls. You were building a—before the BitchSnakeBog
returned—
zenana where your hearts could lounge when one was away at war.

* Cohen, Leonard, *The Future*, "Anthem," 1992.

Disorderly Abecedarian 23: Hidden

Matter of course—the bandaging
water performs for itself, as
jitter of light across its face.

Natter on, says the sand to the waves. We're your
xylophone & no
knotter can tie us together. We're your
zither, say clouds to wind, your
plotters of courses, your
tethers, tenders, traders.
Hotter by the grains of sand, we burn the soles of your
daughter. She swears, "I'll stay back,
even thirsty, or blooded."
                          Waves
chatter—messages foam each to each,
utter what they know, like candles
gutter, burnt-ended, like any
yearning they believe
rather than breaking. They
quiver rather than swim, caught by each
other at the edge, at the edges, which
bother the shores & the banks, which
shatter whatever we know of place, of land. They curl, fall,
love what can't be pure.

Vector of fruit, ice, fish, grain, pulling water up, each
another tideline, where the people bathe & fall. Water
interred between grains of shell, glass, bones, coral, crystal.
Familiar, this is where I have hidden the skins.

Proper Abecedarian 23: January

Another bandage, another look-every-stranger-in-the-eyes, another
bothering to breathe your own city's lights or another's
chattering away about new years & old sins, old beauties, old streets. Another
daughter wears a ring & light.

Either there is breath, or not. Light, or not. Grace, or not.
Familiar as breath & light—grace. Yet you let it be
guttered like the candles after mass. But
hotter than your angry-at-nothing heart, ready with a shovel. Wind alone
inters all the previous year: dispersal=burial. You scribe up the count,
jitter toward the new one. She's two-faced, two-mouthed,
knotter of rages, tangler of warnings, snarler of lashes. She's
lurch from failure to faint, kickshaw to nice, gravity to grace.

Matter is a house for time. Or grace.
Natter is a prayer for blindness. Or grace.
Other is a trap for loathing. Or grace is
plotter, a calendar, an arc, a spark
quivering in the longest nights. You sleep
rather than speak to your familiar, your pen, your
shattered mirror. What you love
tethers you. Pray it holds you while the dark
utters its knives. Pray the sun's needles
vector through all the wounds, stitching the dark closed each breaking day.

Water becomes breath & slip, falls as harmless. The church's ribs become
xylophone—toy on which you learn your notes. Grace
yearns for your throat, or a pen. Air
zithers against your skin—rough tongues of angels licking the hard-born year
    alive.

Disorderly Abecedarian 24: Wedded

For Seamus

1.
Your body—keel and fo'c's'le, bowsprit and quarter-gallery—
buoys mine—rigging
monkey-mad-mushy-love.
Zounds, you swashbuckle me.

Unfailing love of mine, all
heterodoxy & darkened oars.
Giant, this heart, this billowing, this
slew of sloughing off of garment & thinned skin.
Queue me up like cargo, loading & unloading.
Dump me deep in your sheets, darling.

2.
Whole berries squash themselves between our bellies, birds loose
feathers for our toes' wriggling. We were, from our singularities,
xenodochial, non-parochial, matrimonial. You're the
roundabout with exits and entrances glowing in hundreds
I never want to exit, the
effusive floral arrangement of my heart, the
candle in my wind, the
nitwit in my knit, the
pretty in my pretense, my
venom-lancer, claw-puller, lash-dodger, my
terrace-with-a-view-&-foot massages, my
alabaster pillow, my
oxymoron of Jesuit & Franciscan, my being's
knee, my destroyer, my cruiser, my indomitable
love, my lapidary love, my unsleeved heart, my declension, my
jewel-box song, playing even when the lid's closed.

Xenodochial (adjective), friendly to strangers.

Proper Abecedarian 24: To-Do

Alabaster, like paper, comes in other shades, but both conjure *white.*
Buoy can be both warning & elation.
Candle is both object & measurement (lumens). But a to-do list is always a
dump into which
effusions of hope, greed, good intention, self-salvation
feather themselves out like letters turning into flocks. I
grant myself permission to not do the things in order—which should help,
heterodoxy being my natural mode,
ill-got though mode & moderator might be. Still, it's bound to be
jewel among lists, my between-semesters-optimism. Bullshit.

Knee it in its groin &/or kneel before it. Neither works.
Linger over its construction as if it were sestina, or me
monkey digging with a stick for delicious ants.
Nitwit. The bi-annual exercise in futurity is itself
oxymoron: to-do. . .LIST,

Pretty sure the only thing done will have been words on a page,
queue where every time someone gets on the bus, another schlub joins the line,
roundabout without road-signs & the same convenience store at each cardinal
        point,
slew of improvements doomed to molder on the page while I'm
terrace-comfy with scotch/rocks in a mug & a mystery novel.

Unfailing, my knowledge of what wants doing. And my supply of
venom for each new day's bright, fuzzy start.
Whole enterprise is ritual void of real presence.
Xenodochial necessities (friends & relations) kill off what intentions inertia
        doesn't. Look,
yard—onion grass rampant and inedible, flowering and getting more done
        than I.

Zounds! Desk eats page! Squirrels scratch out seeds! Some get satisfied. . .

Disorderly Abecedarian 25: Quaking

Momentarily, I will find myself
grommeting myself to the fabric of Perfection, holding it open for the ropes &
    rods, or
fixing myself to some kiplingesque sticking point, located like
belief in the window/sail/pasture-I-built-for-it.
Love, was it, wove the walls? By glazing by thread by stone? Or
xenomancy—each alien face in which I see belief or jesus or light?

Anent this divination of divine-ation: be not
wasters of light, howsome ever it pours. Even your most oppositional thumb,
    sorest
knuckle, the light that burst from light. In your
yaw & pitch—the breath that broke atoms apart. In your
north, the pull of every compass. In your
south, the tug of eros, eros, eros, longing.

Object, if you will. Mention the blood on our hands, on the Universe's. Mention
cattleprod & flail & switch, the mis-heard
Divine singing songs only trees/numbers/atoms hear correct. Mention how we
quake before our own questions. Mention folly, fumbling,
zaniness, sane-ness. Fill the chalices full of
vermouth you've spiked with wormwood. Drag forth the baskets of questionable
halibut. We'll make a meal of anything. We'll
poke at wounds & clues & plots & salads, clutching the
ephemeral, except nothing but our clutching is ephemeral—all here all along,
unbeknownst to me, at least, until the lights dimmed but never left. My heart's

retrograde again, stuttering at the stars. Stars both
turbulent & steady as bees. Stars both
indignant & indulgent as mothers. We're
juggling all, always letting ashes go, always gathering pollen in our hands.

Xenomancy (noun), divining past, present, and future in the face of a stranger.

Proper Abecedarian 25: Trawling

Anent memory:
Belief in your version can be
cattle-prod—*this hurt, therefore let's repeat*;
divine—scenery that filled and emptied you at once;
ephemeral—names you lose within seconds;
fixed like a star to every wandering;
grommeted like sail to the mast—always waiting to be moved. Say

halibut & you recall a Nova Scotia kitchen. Say
indignant & you relive every time a parent struck you. Say
juggle & you retrieve each time you dropped a ball. Say
knuckle & you remember your father's hands. They

lunge at each other, branching, scrabbling,
momentarily hooking each to each, running
north toward the surface of the brain.
Object though the more practical-minded might, every object
pokes itself toward some past moment—meaningless or so full you
quake with presence. The just-get-on-with-life tribe claims it's
retrograde melody & clogs the song—sends things
south toward your feet, which bleed and stop.

Turbulent, this business of knitting all the fractal threads into one coat.
Unbeknownst, others recall scenes quite differently, like opinions on how much
vermouth makes a martini, & how much makes it a
waste of perfectly good gin.

Xenomancy—the divination of past, present, & future by gazing at a stranger's
    face might
yaw your head out of your heart. Imagine what
zany party you'd have then—drunk with strangers who knew what you wanted
    to recall. . .

Disorderly Abecedarian 26: Bloodtide

Ongoing: even those with palms held up, suppliant, find
knives in the very air they offer themselves to, & the bloodtide
jams itself against our coast, our skins, again. Again,
dam falls, uncleaned flood carries everylife against everylife. Yet somewhere
panda births twins live, some nation stops whaling. Instead of swallowing
    poison, the ocean's
randy for survival, the forests barely napping between seasons for sex &
    getting. We're just
untoward, with all our thirsts & powers—agriculture, horticulture, apiculture,
    Culture still no
evidence to the contrary. The Maker might have borne all
weight once, for us, for what we/I were about to do: how we'd
mate delight & blood, let curiosity fuck consequence, breed fear & making. My
quadrant's mine, stay out, or else. If my quadrant's
verdant, then the whole thing's fine. The

nether quadrant's its own fire, right? The
clever shall inherit. The
bollixing—not so awful before gunpowder bungled limits. The
index, our index, my index, perhaps your index. . . No one left
fudging the list. What did I do with my one wild and precious life? Held
grudges: 1. Not made of gossamer. 2. Not able to fix my parents. 3. Not noisy
    enough.
Title: *Every One Loses Something & It's Never Enough to Stop the Raised Hands.*

Hobble along hobbled. Never get away.
Agonize all you want. It all goes on within you or without you. The sun's still
    a bright
yolk in the egg of the sky, frying itself. Blood on night streets mimics
zinfandel spilling itself into the glass of the world.
Love is 40 pounds of explosive in Allah's desert.
Xeriscape your own heart. It will still bloom when the rains come.

Skein your own heart; stitch by stitch, knit into shrouds or baby blankets. There's enough.

Proper Abecedarian 26: Embrace

Agonize about it: who will touch who & where & when.
Bollix it up by saying "no" when you long to say "help me" to someone's
clever tongue/hips/fingers. Whoever breaches The
Dam of Politeness, piled-on cringing, mortared stricture
evidences the swell of some organ (brain, heart, longing) breaking open
fridge in which she/he has been preserving
grudges & dirges from the last time things went badly, were
hobbled by weariness or lack of wholly charming underwear,
index of body/spirit/history flaws
jamming up The Works, even if you need the works.
Knives don't cut like bad kisses.

Lighten up, dear heart, every peach half has its
mate, & neither gets to keep the seed. The
nethers are for swelling, & juices for
ongoing sweetness, & even the famously hesitant
panda conceives of breaching, being breached. Choose your
quadrant for disrobing: shoulder, shoulder, knee, knee. Throat. Center.

Randy is as concupiscence does. Oh, do.
Skein me like silk, until I'm weave-able.
Title me like a book whose covers spread, whose pages you'll starve without.
Untoward, be, oh, untoward with your fingers, unfurl me
verdant & electric as new growth.

Weight my breath with your breath on my skin. I am not meant for
xeriscaping, drought resistance, cold-season hardiness. Let me be that
yolk you tap your spoon against a shell to reach, that
zinfandel you roll around your tongue. It is ordained.

www.ingramcontent.com/pod-product-compliance
Lightning Source LLC
LaVergne TN
LVHW021617080426
835510LV00019B/2617